THE ZEN OF WORK

Transforming the Tension in Your
Brain, Body, and Business

SHARON GROSSMAN. PHD

WARRIOR
PUBLISHING

ISBN: 978-1-952437-04-5

Contents

CHAPTER 1

Running on Empty

The alarm blared at 5:30 AM, jolting Alex from a fitful sleep. He groaned, fumbling to silence the noise. Another night of tossing and turning, his mind racing with deadlines and to-do lists.

Why can't I just turn it off? The thought spiraled in his head, a reminder of how out of control he felt.

Alex shuffled to the kitchen, making a beeline for the coffee maker. As the rich aroma filled the air, he felt the first spark of life return to his weary body. One sip. Two sips. By the third, his brain fog began to lift, but the familiar knot of anxiety tightened in his stomach. "What fresh chaos awaits me today?" he wondered to himself. "Shower. Suit. Briefcase. Go," he muttered, his daily mantra, a flimsy shield against the day ahead.

The commute was a blur of brake lights and honking horns. Alex's shoulders crept higher, tension coiling in his neck. "I should be grateful for this job," he reminded himself, but gratitude felt like a distant memory. By the time he reached his office, his jaw ached from clenching. Emails. Meetings. Phone calls. Lunch inhaled at his desk, a mere pit stop in the relentless grind.

"Alex, we need those projections by EOD."

"Alex, can you hop on a quick call?"

"Alex, got a minute?" He didn't have a minute. He didn't have a second to spare. But he nodded and smiled, "Of course."

"Why do they all look to me? What if I fail them?"

The questions haunted him, each one a reminder of his inadequacy. He felt like a hamster on a wheel, running faster and faster but staying in one place. His once-vibrant spirit was dwindling, replaced by a gnawing sense of emptiness. He missed the simple joys of life—a leisurely walk in the park, a quiet evening at home with his wife Olivia, the feeling of accomplishment after completing a meaningful task.

The pressure was relentless. His boss seemed to have an insatiable appetite for work, demanding more, more, more.

"What if I can't deliver?"

"You're not good enough."

"You'll be exposed."

These thoughts echoed in his head, robbing him of rest. His appetite was erratic, swinging between ravenous hunger and complete disinterest. He found himself reaching for unhealthy comfort foods, indulging in sugary snacks and greasy takeout, trying to fill a void that only seemed to grow.

The more poorly he ate, the worse he felt. The worse he felt, the less likely he was to exercise. Alex was trapped in a vicious cycle.

As the clock ticked away, Alex's sense of urgency grew. He tried to focus, but his mind was racing. By the end of the day, he realized with a sinking feeling that he had barely made a dent in his workload.

As the sun dipped below the horizon, casting long shadows across his cluttered desk, Alex finally let out a breath he hadn't realized he was holding.

Exhausted and deflated, he gathered his things and headed home.

Olivia's warm smile greeted him at the door, a beacon in the storm of his day. "Rough day?" she asked, concern in her eyes. Alex nodded, collapsing onto the couch. "I don't know how much longer I can do this, Liv."

She sat beside him, taking his hand. "Maybe it's time for a break. A real one."

"I can't just leave everything," Alex protested weakly, the weight of his responsibilities pressing down on him.

"You can't keep going like this either," Olivia countered. "What about that retreat center we saw? The one in Guatemala by the lake?"

Alex hesitated for a long moment. It was beautiful and inviting, he remembered. What if he went there? Would it really make a difference? Would it be worth it? What about all the work that would accumulate while he was gone?

But deep down inside, he knew it was the right choice. He'd have to figure the rest out.

Alex reached for his laptop. His fingers flew across the keys: "burnout retreat transformation." There it was. A secluded lodge. Maximum five participants. "Reconnect with your passion and purpose." Starting in eight days.

He looked at Olivia, a glimmer of hope in his tired eyes. Could this be the answer?

She squeezed his hand. "Go. Find yourself again. I'll be here when you get back. It's just one week."

Alex took a deep breath and clicked "Book Now."

CHAPTER 2

The Journey Begins

Alex stared out the window of the plane as it descended into Mexico City, the sprawling metropolis stretching as far as the eye could see. His body ached from the cramped seat, and his mind buzzed with the constant hum of unfinished tasks. "What am I doing?" he thought, not for the first time since leaving his office in Menlo Park. His journey to Guatemala was far from over, but this stopover in Mexico City was a stark reminder of the distance he'd traveled and the adventure that lay ahead.

The idea of a retreat had seemed appealing in theory—a chance to recharge, to escape the relentless pace of Silicon Valley. But now, as he faced the reality of disconnecting, anxiety preyed on his mind. "How bad can it be?" he reassured himself.

"Worst case, I'll just hole up in my room with a book." He couldn't remember the last time he'd read something that wasn't a quarterly report or an urgent email.

Mexico City's airport was a cacophony of sounds and smells. Alex's head throbbed as he navigated the crowded terminals, his carry-on bag suddenly feeling like a dead weight. He'd managed only three hours of sleep on the flight, and it showed in the dark circles under his eyes and the slump of his shoulders.

Security was a nightmare. Alex found himself in a line that seemed to stretch for miles, surrounded by impatient travelers and crying babies. By the time he made it through, his nerves were frayed. He sprinted towards his gate, only to realize with growing horror that he couldn't find his boarding pass for the connecting flight to Guatemala.

Panic rose in his throat as he frantically searched his pockets, his bag, retracing his steps. The minutes ticked by, and with each passing moment, his chance of making the flight dwindled. Finally, defeated, he approached the counter.

"I'm sorry, sir," the attendant said, her voice tinged with sympathy. "That flight has already departed. We can get you on the next one, but there's a rebooking fee."

Alex nodded numbly, reaching for his wallet. He handed over his credit card, only to hear the dreaded words: "I'm sorry, but your card has been declined."

It was the final straw. Alex felt something inside him snap. His face flushed red, and he could hear his pulse pounding in his ears. "This is ridiculous!" he exploded, his voice rising. "I'm trying to go on a damn retreat to relax, and I can't even get there without everything falling apart!"

"Breathe," a calm voice said from behind him. Alex turned to see a woman in her fifties, her silver hair elegantly styled, a serene smile on her face. "Mercury must be in retrograde or something. I missed my connection too—security was a beast."

Alex felt some of the tension drain from his body as Samantha, a fellow retreat attendee, assisted him with calling his credit card company to let them know he was out of the country so he could rebook his flight. "We're going to the same retreat," she explained. "I've already arranged for the driver to wait for us in Guatemala City."

As they sat at the gate, waiting for their new flight, Alex found himself opening up to Samantha. There was something about her calm demeanor that put him at ease. For the first time since leaving California, he felt a glimmer of hope. Maybe this retreat wouldn't be so bad after all.

Hours later, as their small plane touched down in Guatemala, Alex's first glimpse of the verdant countryside took his breath away. The air was thick with humidity and the scent of tropical flowers. As promised, a driver waited for them, holding a sign with their names.

As Alex and Samantha climbed into the shuttle, they found three other passengers already seated, waiting patiently. Marcus, a sharp-suited executive with an air of impatience, was tapping away at his phone, his brow furrowed in concentration. Beside him sat Taylor, arms crossed and lips pursed in a skeptical frown, eyeing the newcomers with a mix of curiosity and suspicion. In stark contrast, Raj occupied the back row, his vibrant shirt a splash of color against the shuttle's muted interior. He greeted Alex and Samantha with an enthusiastic wave, his eyes sparkling with an energy that seemed at odds with the retreat's promise of relaxation.

As the shuttle pulled away from the curb, Alex couldn't help but wonder how this eclectic group would mesh over the coming days, each of them clearly bringing their own expectations and reservations.

The drive to the retreat stretched on for three long hours, winding through city streets that seemed to pulse with life. As the shuttle traversed narrow roads, Alex gazed out at the billboards, the people, and the cars. What had he gotten himself into?

Samantha chatted with Marcus about their respective careers, while Taylor sat quietly, her arms still crossed, a skeptical expression etched on her face. Raj, on the other hand, animatedly shared stories of his entrepreneurial ventures, his voice rising and falling with excitement. Alex listened, trying to absorb the energy of the group, but his thoughts kept drifting back to the stress he had left behind.

Finally, they reached the lakeshore, where a small boat awaited them, bobbing gently on the water. The sun descended lower in the sky, casting a golden glow over the lake. As they boarded, the driver helped them stow their bags, and soon they were gliding across the water, the gentle lapping of waves soothing Alex's frayed nerves.

The boat ride was a refreshing change, the cool breeze ruffling his hair and the scent of the lake filling his lungs. As the minutes passed, the sky darkened, and the first stars began to twinkle above.

The retreat was located on an island, and as they approached, the outline of the lodge emerged from the shadows, illuminated by soft, welcoming lights. It looked like a scene from a dream, a sanctuary nestled in the heart of nature.

Once they docked, the group disembarked, their exhaustion palpable. Alex could feel his stomach growling, a reminder that he hadn't eaten since the hasty snack at the airport.

They hurried through the entrance, where a friendly staff member greeted them with warm smiles and a refreshing drink. "Welcome to Oasis del Sol!" she said, her voice cheerful. "Let's get you checked in."

All Alex could think about was putting his bags down and heading straight to dinner. The thought of finally relaxing and enjoying a meal felt like a much-needed respite.

As they completed the check-in process, another staff member greeted them with a warm smile and handed each of them a cool, fragrant towel. The sensation of the damp cloth against his skin was instantly refreshing, and Alex felt some of the day's tension begin to melt away.

"You're just in time for the welcome circle," she said, her voice soothing and melodious. "But first, let's show you to your rooms so you can freshen up."

Despite his biting hunger, Alex felt a wave of relief at the thought of a moment to himself. They were led down a winding path, the soft glow of lanterns illuminating their way. The night air was thick with the scent of tropical flowers and the distant sound of lapping waves.

Alex's room was simple but comfortable, with large windows that looked out over the moonlit lake. The presence of the hammock on his patio reminded him that this was his chance to rest and recharge. He quickly splashed water on his face and changed his shirt, grateful for the chance to shed the grime of travel. As he caught sight of himself in the mirror, he paused. He looked tired, yes, but there was something else there too—a hint of curiosity, maybe even excitement. How bad can it be? he thought again, this time with a small smile.

He took a deep breath, inhaling the scent of jasmine that drifted in through the open window. The tranquility of the setting was already beginning to work its magic.

A gentle knock at the door reminded him of the waiting welcome circle and dinner beyond. The urgency of his hunger had softened, replaced by a growing sense of anticipation. Then, squaring his shoulders, he stepped out to join the others.

As they made their way to the introductory gathering, Alex found himself walking between Samantha and Raj, their presence oddly comforting. The path opened up to the wooden dock, dimly lit, surrounded by the water that brought him there, and ever so serene. At its center, he could see the other retreat participants gathering.

Alex took another deep breath, feeling more ready — or as ready as he could be — to begin this strange new adventure. Whatever lay ahead, at least it would be different from the relentless grind he'd left behind. And right now, different felt like exactly what he needed.

CHAPTER 3

Embracing the Unfamiliar

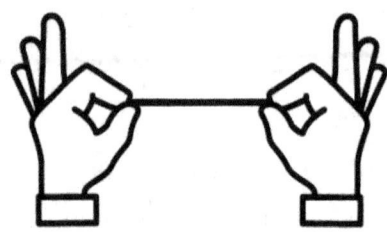

The welcome circle at Oasis del Sol was unlike anything Alex had ever experienced. As he sat cross-legged on a cushion, surrounded by strangers, he felt distinctly out of place. The retreat leader, Elena, a serene woman with kind eyes, encouraged them to share their intentions for the week ahead.

Alex listened as the others spoke. Samantha hoped to reconnect with her inner wisdom. Raj wanted to spark his creativity. Taylor grudgingly admitted she needed to "chill out." Marcus said, "Frankly, I'm not entirely sure what I'm doing here. I mean, I've got a company to run, deals to close, and a reputation to uphold. But I suppose a little downtime couldn't hurt. Maybe I can figure out how to actually relax without feeling guilty about it." When it was Alex's turn, he hesitated. "I... I guess I'm here to let off some steam," he said, the words feeling foreign on his tongue.

Dinner followed, a vegetarian feast that surprised Alex with its flavors and textures. As he savored each bite, he realized how long it had been since he'd truly tasted his food, instead of inhaling it between meetings or in front of his computer.

DAY 1

The next morning at 6 AM, Alex found himself in the yoga hall, a stunning domed structure with floor-to-ceiling windows that overlooked the shimmering lake. The early light filtered through, casting a soft glow across the room and illuminating the tranquil waters. On the other side of the lake, three majestic volcanoes rose like ancient guardians, their silhouettes framed against the pastel sky.

As the participants settled onto their floor cushions, Elena invited them to engage in an open-eye meditation. "This practice allows us to connect with our surroundings while remaining present within ourselves," she explained, her voice calm and soothing.

Alex felt a flutter of skepticism. "How could I meditate with my eyes open?" But he followed the group's lead, allowing his gaze to soften as he took in the breathtaking view. As he focused on the distant volcanoes, he felt the tears welling up inside him, an unexpected rush of gratitude flooding his heart.

"This place is beautiful," he thought, overwhelmed by the serenity that surrounded him. For the first time in what felt like ages, he was able to leave his chaotic world behind, if only for a few days. The gentle sounds of nature—the rustling leaves, the soft lapping of water against the shore—wrapped around him like a warm embrace. In this moment, he realized he had time for himself, truly. No emails, no meetings, just the soothing presence of the lake and the mountains.

Elena guided them through the meditation, encouraging them to notice their breath and the sensations in their bodies while maintaining a relaxed gaze. Alex found himself drawn deeper into the experience, the beauty of the landscape merging with his inner landscape. Each breath felt like a release, each moment a step further away from the stress that had consumed him for so long.

As the meditation came to a close, Alex opened his eyes fully, blinking against the brightness of the day. He felt lighter, as if a weight had been lifted from his shoulders. The tears that had threatened to spill were now replaced with a sense of calm determination.

After the meditation, the group moved to the dining area for breakfast. The nourishing food, prepared with fresh, local ingredients, further fueled Alex's sense of renewal. As he savored each bite, he found himself contemplating the day ahead. The schedule for the rest of the day was largely open, save for one appointment he knew was coming: a massage at 11 AM. This single known element in a sea of unknowns both comforted and intrigued him. He wondered what other experiences awaited him in the coming hours and days.

The unknown, which had always been a source of anxiety for Alex, now held a glimmer of possibility. His journey at Oasis del Sol was just beginning, and each moment held the potential for discovery and transformation. With a deep breath, Alex stood up from the table, ready to embrace whatever the retreat had in store for him. As he walked back to his room, he realized that for the first time in a long time, he has time to spare. He could lounge on his hammock, read a book, go for a walk. The possibilities were inviting, enticing, and he felt a newfound lightness in his steps. Perhaps this retreat would indeed be the turning point he so desperately needed.

CHAPTER 4

Unraveling Tension

As Alex entered the spa at Oasis del Sol, the soothing scent of lavender and the soft sound of trickling water immediately enveloped him. He was here for his 11 AM massage, the one appointment he'd been both anticipating and slightly dreading.

The massage therapist, Maria, greeted him with a warm smile. "Welcome, Alex," she said, her Spanish accent coming across. "How are you feeling today?"

"Fine," Alex replied automatically, then paused. "Actually, I'm not sure. A bit overwhelmed, I guess."

Maria nodded understandingly. "That's okay. Let's see what your body has to say."

As Alex lay face down on the massage table, he tried to relax, but found his mind racing as usual. Maria began with gentle strokes across his back, and Alex winced as she hit a particularly tight spot between his shoulder blades.

"You're carrying a lot of tension here," Maria observed, her fingers working skillfully to loosen the knot. "Try to breathe into it."

Alex attempted to focus on his breath, but found it challenging. As Maria continued her work, moving from his back to his shoulders and neck, Alex was struck by how much discomfort he felt. Each area she touched seemed to be a new discovery of tension he hadn't even realized was there.

"Your body is like a map of your stress," Maria said softly. "These knots and tight spots tell a story."

As she worked on a particularly stubborn knot in his lower back, Alex felt a sudden rush of emotion. It was as if the physical release of tension was unlocking something deeper. He realized, with a start, that it wasn't just his mind that had been wound tight all these years - his body had been silently bearing the burden as well.

"It's okay to let go," Maria encouraged, sensing his emotional shift. "Your body has been holding onto this for a long time."

Alex's eyes welled up with tears. He'd always prided himself on his ability to handle stress, to push through and get things done. But now, as Maria's hands worked to release years of accumulated tension, he realized the toll it had taken on his physical self.

As the massage continued, Alex found himself becoming more aware of his body. He noticed how his breath had been shallow and constricted, and made a conscious effort to breathe more deeply. With each exhale, he felt a little more of the tension melting away.

By the end of the session, Alex felt both exhausted and oddly energized. As he sat up, he caught sight of himself in a mirror across the room. His posture seemed different - more open, less guarded.

"How do you feel, Mr. Alex?" Maria asked.

"Like I've just woken up," Alex replied, surprised by his own answer. "I had no idea I was carrying so much... stuff in my body."

Maria smiled. "Our bodies and minds are deeply connected. When we neglect one, the other suffers too."

As Alex left the spa, he felt a newfound respect for his physical self. He realized that true well-being wasn't just about managing his thoughts or his work schedule - it was about honoring the needs of his body as well.

Walking back to his room, Alex felt a sense of lightness he hadn't experienced in years. The tension in his muscles had eased, but more importantly, he'd gained a new awareness. He made a mental note to pay more attention to his body's signals going forward.

As he reached his room, Alex paused at the door. For the first time in a long while, he felt truly present in his own skin. It was a small step, but it felt like the beginning of something significant. With this new bodily awareness, he wondered what other revelations the retreat might bring.

This retreat was, in fact, unlike anything Alex had ever encountered, and he wanted to ensure he didn't forget the insights he was gaining.

He settled into a cozy chair on the balcony, overlooking the tranquil lake. The sun sparkled on the water, and the distant volcanoes stood like ancient sentinels. He pulled out his journal, a simple leather-bound book that felt foreign yet inviting in his hands.

As he opened it, he felt a wave of vulnerability wash over him. "What do I even write?" he thought. But he pushed through the uncertainty and began his first entry.

Journal Entry: Day 1 at Oasis del Sol

Today was a whirlwind. I woke up at dawn. The meditation session was unlike anything I've ever experienced. I found myself overwhelmed by gratitude and a sense of peace as I gazed at the volcanoes.

The massage at 11 AM was a revelation. I've always thought of myself as someone who can handle stress, but the tension in my body was a stark reminder of how much I've been holding onto. Maria's skilled hands worked wonders, and I felt a wave of emotion as the knots in my muscles began to release. It was like my body was finally speaking up, telling me that I needed to slow down and take better care of myself.

I'm starting to see a connection between my physical and mental states. I've always been so focused on my mind, on productivity and achieving goals. But today, I realized that neglecting my body has taken a toll on my overall well-being. I'm determined to make a conscious effort to listen to my body's signals and take better care of myself.

I'm starting to understand why people come to places like this. It's not just about relaxation; it's about a deep sense of renewal. I feel lighter, more present, and more connected to myself. I'm excited to see what the rest of the retreat has in store.

CHAPTER 5

The Art of Slowing Down

Alex entered the yoga hall, his muscles still tingling from yesterday's massage. The room was bathed in soft morning light, and the scent of incense hung in the air. As he unrolled his mat, he noticed the other retreat participants settling in around him.

Elena, the yoga instructor, sat at the front of the room, her serene presence immediately calming the space. "Welcome to Yin yoga," she began, her voice soft but clear. "This practice is about slowing down, about finding stillness in both body and mind."

Alex shifted uncomfortably on his mat. Slowing down wasn't exactly his forte. He glanced around, noticing Marcus checking his watch impatiently, while Samantha closed her eyes, seeming to embrace the calm atmosphere.

"We'll start with deep breaths," Elena continued. "Focus your mind on a single point - your breath. This one-pointed focus unlocks tension in the brain."

As they began to breathe deeply, Alex found his mind wandering to his endless to-do list. He forced himself to redirect his attention to his breath, surprised at how challenging it was to maintain focus.

"Now, we'll move into our first pose," Elena instructed. "Remember, in Yin yoga, we hold poses for longer periods, about 3-5 minutes each. The asanas, or movements, unlock tension in the body, just as the breath unlocks tension in the mind."

As they eased into a seated forward fold, Alex felt the familiar urge to push harder, to stretch further. But Elena's gentle reminder echoed in the room: "Yin is active, but not that active. We're not here to force or strain. It's more of a passive stretching."

Alex noticed Taylor fidgeting nearby, clearly as uncomfortable with the slow pace as he was. Raj, on the other hand, seemed to melt into each pose with ease, his face a picture of contentment.

"If you work your body too much," Elena explained, "it speaks to you through tightness. When something is tight, we have a tendency not to hold it as long. But here, we practice patience. It moves us closer to balance. I invite you to go inwards. Just notice the tension and sit with it. What you'll find is that it will shift."

As they transitioned into a hip-opening pose, Alex felt a deep stretch in his tight IT bands. His instinct was to come out of the pose immediately, but Elena's words resonated with him. He took a deep breath and tried to settle into the discomfort.

Across the room, Marcus let out an audible sigh of frustration. Alex caught Samantha sending him a sympathetic smile. It was clear they were all struggling in their own ways with the slow, deliberate nature of the practice.

As the class progressed, moving through increasingly deeper postures, Alex found himself surprised by the intensity of the practice. Despite the slow pace, he could feel his muscles working, stretching in ways they hadn't before.

"Remember," Elena said as they held a particularly challenging pose, "patience is key. We're not trying to achieve anything here. We're simply being present with our bodies, with our breath."

By the end of the class, Alex felt a strange mix of relaxation and restlessness. His body felt looser, more open, but his mind was still racing, trying to process the new experience.

As they rolled up their mats, Alex overheard snippets of conversation. Marcus was complaining about the "waste of time," while Raj was enthusiastically describing the "profound stillness" he'd experienced. Taylor seemed conflicted, admitting it was challenging but also acknowledging feeling more relaxed than she had in years.

Alex remained quiet, still processing. As he left the yoga hall, he caught Elena's eye. She gave him a knowing smile. "How did you find it?" she asked.

"Challenging," Alex admitted. "But... interesting. I think I have a lot to learn about slowing down."

Elena nodded. "That's a great place to start. Remember, Yin yoga isn't about achieving or doing. It's about being. Give it time."

As Alex walked back to his room, he found himself pondering Elena's words. The idea of "being" rather than "doing" was foreign to him, but he couldn't deny the subtle shift he felt in his body and mind.

Maybe, he thought, there was something to this slowing down after all.

Journal Entry: Day 2 at Oasis del Sol

The Yin yoga class this morning was a revelation. The pace was so different from anything I've ever done. I've always been used to pushing myself, to working hard and fast. But here, I had to slow down and really feel each pose. It was challenging. I struggled to hold the postures, and my mind kept racing with thoughts about work and life back home. Yet, as I focused on my breath, I began to understand the beauty of patience.

Elena taught us that deep breathing creates a one-pointed mind, helping to unlock tension in the brain. The asanas, or movements, unlock tension in the body. I felt the tightness in my hips and lower back, and for the first time, I allowed myself to sit with that discomfort instead of running from it.

I realize now that if I work my body too much, it speaks to me through tightness. I've been so focused on achieving that I've neglected the importance of balance. This retreat is teaching me that it's okay to be still, to be patient.

As I sit here, I want to savor this experience. I want to remember how it feels to be present, to breathe deeply, and to connect with my body. I hope to carry this awareness back home with me, to integrate it into my daily life.

Alex paused, looking out at the lake, feeling a warmth spread through him. He was grateful for this time away, for the opportunity to reflect and grow. The act of journaling was already proving to be a powerful tool for capturing his thoughts and emotions.

He closed the journal, feeling a sense of accomplishment. This was just the beginning, but he was ready to embrace whatever came next. As he stood up and stretched, he felt a little lighter, a little more open. The journey ahead was still uncertain, but for the first time in a long while, he felt hopeful.

CHAPTER 6

The Edge of Tension

On the third day of the retreat, Alex found himself back in the yoga hall, settling onto his mat for another Yin yoga session. The room was filled with a quiet anticipation as Elena took her place at the front.

"Today," Elena began, her voice soft yet clear, "we're going to explore the concept of 'passively hunting for the cutting edge of tension.' This means gently pushing until you feel challenged, but not overwhelmed."

As they moved into a figure 4 pose on their backs, Elena encouraged them to experiment. "Try some gentle rocking," she suggested. "If you're at a 9 in terms of intensity, wait until you reach a 6 or 7 before going deeper. Then, mindfully move it up to an 8."

Alex closed his eyes, focusing on the sensation in his hip. He rocked gently, feeling the stretch intensify and then ease. As he waited for the intensity to subside, he noticed Marcus next to him, pushing hard into the pose, his face tense with effort.

"Remember," Elena continued, "there's a law of diminishing returns. Sometimes reaching a 6 isn't possible, especially if you don't maintain consistent breathing. Be patient with yourself."

As they transitioned through various poses, Alex observed the others. Samantha seemed to have found her rhythm, moving with a newfound grace. Taylor, usually fidgety, was surprisingly still, her face a mask of concentration. Raj, as always, appeared completely at ease, a serene smile on his face.

After the class, Alex retreated to his room, feeling contemplative. He pulled out his journal, ready to capture his thoughts.

Journal Entry: Day 3 at Oasis del Sol

Today's yoga session was eye-opening. The concept of "passively hunting for the cutting edge of tension" resonated deeply with me. It made me realize how I typically push myself too hard in every aspect of my life. I'm always at a 9 or 10, never giving myself the chance to ease back and find a more sustainable level of effort.

This gentle approach to challenging oneself is new to me. It's a reminder that going slow doesn't mean it's not challenging. In fact, I found it even more difficult because I wasn't rushing through. I had to be mindful and endure the challenge longer. It's about tuning into the moment, really feeling what's happening in my body.

I'm starting to see how this applies beyond yoga. In my work, I'm always rushing from one task to the next. But what if I approached my projects the way we approached the poses today? Gently pushing to the edge, then easing back, finding a sustainable rhythm. It's counterintuitive, but I think it might actually lead to better results and less burnout.

I'm learning that true strength isn't about constant intensity, but about finding balance and sustainability.

Alex closed his journal. For the first time in years, he felt truly present in the moment, aware of his body, his breath, and his surroundings. He could see how this awareness was a powerful tool and was determined to carry it with him long after the retreat ended.

CHAPTER 7

Deepening Connections

Alex found himself sitting on the yoga mat yet again, his body folded over his legs in a butterfly pose. The room was quiet except for the sound of steady breathing and the occasional rustle of moving bodies. Elena's soothing voice broke the silence.

"As you hold this pose," she began, her tone gentle yet firm, "I want you to think about going deeper. Not just physically, but mentally and emotionally as well."

Alex felt a twinge in his lower back and resisted the urge to come out of the pose. He focused on his breath, trying to sink further into the stretch.

"In yoga, as in life," Elena continued, "everything is about establishing a deeper level of connection. Once you find this deeper connection, it becomes almost addictive. You start craving it in every aspect of your life."

She paused, allowing her words to sink in. Alex found his mind wandering to his work back home, wondering what a deeper connection might look like there.

"Everything you do needs to have deeper meaning," Elena said, as if reading his thoughts. "From the food you eat to the people you talk to. It's about being fully present and engaged in every moment."

As they transitioned to a new pose, Elena encouraged them to explore their sensations. "If you don't feel much, go further and hunt for the sensation. Once you find it, move into the relationship with that tension. When it shifts, go to the next layer. There's always a deeper level to explore."

Alex closed his eyes, focusing intently on the stretch in his hip. It felt tight, no doubt. But he imagined pushing past the initial discomfort, searching for a deeper sensation. To his surprise, he found it - a subtle shift that allowed him to go to the next layer of depth.

As the class progressed, Elena's words continued to resonate. "This practice of hunting for sensation, of constantly seeking a deeper connection - it's not just about yoga. It's a metaphor for life. When you feel stagnant or bored, it's a sign to go deeper, to search for purpose and meaning."

By the time the class ended, Alex felt not only physically stretched but mentally expanded.

As the class dispersed, Raj caught Alex's eye. "Fancy a dip in the lake?" he asked with a grin. Alex nodded, grateful for the company and the chance to cool off.

The water was refreshing, a stark contrast to the humid air. As they swam, Raj began to share his thoughts on the morning's lesson. "You know," Raj said, treading water, "this whole concept of slowing down and deepening connections - it's changed my entire approach to life and business."

Alex raised an eyebrow, intrigued. "How so?"

Raj's eyes lit up. "Well, take my company for instance. I used to be all about rapid growth, constantly chasing the next big thing. But after I started practicing Yin, I realized the power of going slower, of really connecting with what I'm doing."

They swam to shallower water where they could stand. Raj continued, "Now, I take time to truly understand each project, each client. I've even changed how I eat and who I spend time with. It's all about finding deeper meaning in everything."

Alex nodded, thinking about his own frantic pace back home. "But doesn't that slow you down? How do you stay competitive?"

Raj laughed. "That's the beauty of it, Alex. By slowing down, I've actually become more effective. My team is more engaged, our products are better, and our clients are happier. It's like Elena said - it's about hunting for that deeper sensation, that purpose. And I find that when I take more time, I connect more deeply to my employees and my customers. I understand them better and everyone wins."

As they dried off on the shore, Alex felt a spark of inspiration. "So, how do you apply this to your daily life?"

"It's about being present in every moment," Raj explained. "When I'm in a meeting, I'm fully there, listening deeply. I take notes, reflect back the main points to ensure I heard the person right. This makes them feel appreciated and valued. And when I'm working on a problem, I don't rush to the first solution - I sit with it, explore it from all angles."

Alex nodded, his mind racing with possibilities. "I can see how that could be powerful. But it's so different from how I've always operated."

Raj clapped him on the shoulder. "That's the challenge, my friend. But trust me, it's worth it. Start small - maybe with how you approach your next project or even just how you have your next conversation."

As they walked back to their rooms, Alex felt a sense of excitement he hadn't experienced in years. He had a lot to think about. Back in his room, Alex pulled out his journal, eager to capture his thoughts.

Journal Entry: Day 4 at Oasis del Sol

Today's Yin yoga class and my conversation with Raj have opened up a whole new perspective for me. The idea of slowing down to actually go deeper and achieve more is counterintuitive to everything I've believed about success, but I'm starting to see its potential.

Key takeaways:

1. *Deeper connections come from slowing down*

2. *Everything should have deeper meaning - from the food I eat to the people I talk to*

3. *If I'm not feeling much or am bored (in work or life), I need to go further and "hunt for the sensation" or purpose*

4. *It's about constantly moving into a relationship with tension, then shifting to the next layer*

I'm thinking about how I can apply this when I get back home:

- *In meetings: Really listen, be fully present instead of multitasking*

- *With projects: Take time to explore all angles before rushing to solutions*

- *With my team: Foster deeper connections, understand their motivations and strengths*

- *In my personal life: Be more mindful about my food choices, my conversations, my downtime*

It's daunting to think about changing my approach so dramatically, but I'm excited by the possibilities. What if by slowing down, I could actually achieve more meaningful results? What if I could feel more fulfilled in my work and life?

I'm committed to trying this approach when I return. Maybe I'll start with one meeting, one project, one meal at a time. It's about building a new relationship with time and purpose.

Raj's success story is inspiring. If he can transform his business and life through this philosophy, maybe I can too. It's time to go deeper, in every aspect of my life.

Alex closed his journal, curious about where this new path would take him.

CHAPTER 8

A Lesson in Balance

The yoga hall was bathed in soft morning light as Alex found himself in a deep hip opener. His left foot was stretched to the back of the mat, knee lowered, while his right foot rested near his elbows. The stretch was intense, bordering on uncomfortable.

"Now," Elena's soothing voice instructed, "take your block and rest your forehead on it. Allow yourself to relax into the pose."

As Alex followed her guidance and placed his forehead on his block, he was able to surrender into the pose. It became less of a struggle and soon thereafter, he felt a sudden release. The tension in his hip began to melt away, and with it, some of the mental strain he'd been carrying. In this moment of surrender, he realized that sometimes, support wasn't a weakness—it was a tool for growth.

After class, Alex sat next to Marcus at breakfast. The high-powered executive looked as polished as ever, but there was a hint of fatigue in his eyes.

"I don't know about all this 'soft' stuff," Marcus grumbled, stabbing at his fruit salad. "In my world, you push through discomfort. That's how you succeed."

Alex nodded, understanding Marcus's perspective all too well. It had been his own not too long ago. "I used to think the same way," he admitted. "But I'm starting to see things differently."

As they continued their conversation, Alex's mind drifted to Jake, his eager but sometimes struggling direct report back home. He remembered a recent project where Jake had been floundering, clearly out of his depth but too afraid to ask for help.

In that moment, Alex had a revelation. "You know," he said to Marcus, "I'm realizing that good leadership isn't about pushing people to their breaking point. It's about providing the right support so they can push themselves further than they thought possible."

Marcus raised an eyebrow, intrigued. "Go on."

"In yoga today, using the block allowed me to go deeper into the pose than I could have on my own. It wasn't a crutch—it was a tool for growth. I think maybe that's what our teams need from us. Not just pressure, but the right kind of support."

Marcus fell silent, contemplating Alex's words. After a moment, he nodded slowly. "I never thought about it that way."

As they finished their breakfast, Alex excused himself and headed back to his room, eager to capture his thoughts in his journal.

Journal Entry: Day 5 at Oasis del Sol

I'm starting to see a parallel between the yoga mat and the boardroom. In yoga, we made use of the block to go deeper by relaxing into the pose. It made me think about how I support my team through my leadership and how that can help them reach new heights. It's not about doing the work for them, but about providing the tools and guidance they need to push themselves further.

Marcus's reaction to our conversation was interesting. I think he's starting to see the value in this "softer" approach too. It's making me wonder: what if the key to being a truly effective leader isn't about being the toughest or the most driven, but about finding the right balance between challenge and support?

When I get back, I want to have a one-on-one with Jake. I need to understand where he needs support and how I can provide it without taking away his opportunity to grow. Maybe I can be the "block" that helps him reach new heights in his own work.

This retreat is changing me in ways I never expected. I came here looking for a way to manage my stress, but I'm leaving with a whole new perspective on leadership and life.

Despite his excitement, Alex knew that changing ingrained habits wouldn't be easy. Still, he felt truly inspired about the future of his leadership and his team.

CHAPTER 9

The Gift of Discomfort

Today, as they held their yoga poses, Elena's voice flowed through the room, guiding them deeper. "Love the tension," she instructed. "Thank it. It serves a purpose. Some tension is created by stress, and some of that stress is needed stress."

Alex felt a twinge in his lower back and instinctively wanted to pull away from the discomfort. But Elena continued, "Don't brace against the sensation. Go deeper by letting go more. Notice the feeling that comes with it."

As Alex focused on the tension in his body, his mind drifted to a recent encounter with Stephanie, the HR Director back at his company. In his mind's eye, he saw her sitting across from him in the sleek conference room, her expression a mix of support and expectation.

"Alex," Stephanie had said, "your promotion comes with new challenges. The company believes in your potential, but we need you to step up in ways you haven't before."

Back in the present, Elena's voice brought him back to the yoga hall. "Remember, every time you practice, it's different. Embrace that change."

As the class ended, Alex found himself pondering his relationship with stress. He had always viewed tension as something to be eliminated, a sign that he wasn't coping well enough. The idea that it could serve a purpose, that some stress might actually be needed, was a revelation.

He thought about his approach to work - the long hours, the constant push for productivity, the neglect of rest and balance. Had he been fighting against the very thing that could help him grow?

Later, in his room, Alex pulled out his journal, eager to capture his thoughts.

Journal Entry: Day 6 at Oasis del Sol

Today's yoga class challenged me in unexpected ways. The idea of "loving the tension" feels counterintuitive, but it's making me rethink my entire approach to stress and discomfort.

I've always seen tension as the enemy, something to be eliminated at all costs. But what if some of that tension is actually necessary? What if it's pushing me to grow, to adapt, to become better?

I keep thinking about what Stephanie said before I left for this retreat. The company has expectations of me, and I've been so focused on meeting those expectations that I've ignored my own needs for balance and rest. But maybe that tension between what's expected of me and what I need for myself is actually important. Maybe it's telling me something.

I'm starting to see that my approach to work has been unsustainable. I've been all about productivity, pushing myself to the limit, and ignoring the signs that I needed to slow down. But if I can learn to embrace some of that tension, to see it as a tool for growth rather than an obstacle to overcome, maybe I can find a more balanced way of leading.

The challenge now is figuring out how to apply this in real life. How do I distinguish between helpful tension and harmful stress? How do I "love the tension" in my daily work without burning out? How do I let go more?

I guess I could focus less on trying to do everything perfectly and let go of my fear of failure and disappointment. I don't want to completely let go of control because quality really matters to me. But maybe just recalibrate a bit? And what I'm learning, which might be challenging, is to let go of my attachment to the outcome. I've got to be open to change, to face uncertainty because the truth is, I can't really control what happens. I can just direct my mind and my actions toward my goals, but I'll need to release the rest.

It reminds me of what John Lennon once wrote, that "Life is what happens to you while you're busy making other plans."

I need to talk to Olivia about this. She always helps me see things more clearly.

After closing his journal, Alex reached for his phone. He needed to hear Olivia's voice, to share these new insights with her.

"Hey, you," Olivia answered, her voice warm and familiar.

"Liv," Alex began, "I think I'm starting to understand something important here."

As he shared his revelations about tension and stress, Olivia listened attentively. When he finished, she was quiet for a moment.

"That's really interesting, Alex," she said finally. "It sounds like you're learning to see stress in a new light. But remember, embracing tension doesn't mean ignoring your limits. It's about finding the right balance."

Alex nodded, even though she couldn't see him. "You're right. I think that's the key - finding the balance. I've been so far on one end of the spectrum, and now I need to find my way back to the middle."

As they continued to talk, Alex felt a sense of clarity and purpose he hadn't experienced in years. He was grateful for Olivia's steady presence, her ability to ground him even from afar.

When they finally said goodbye, Alex felt ready to face the next phase of his journey. He was beginning to see that true transformation wasn't about eliminating all discomfort, but about learning to dance with it, to use it as a tool for growth and change.

CHAPTER 10

Sweet Reflections

The yoga hall, usually filled with the sound of deep breathing and gentle movements, now buzzed with a different energy. The retreat participants sat in a circle, surrounded by a beautiful arrangement of flowers, crystals, and candles that cast a warm, inviting glow. The air was rich with the aroma of cacao.

Elena sat in the center, a large bowl of melted ceremonial chocolate beside her. "As we come to the end of our journey together," Elena began, her voice warm and melodious, "we'll share in this sacred cacao ceremony. Here in Guatemala, the indigenous people believe that the spirit of sacred cacao can elevate our awareness while connecting us to our true nature. As you taste the richness of the chocolate, reflect on the richness of your experience here. When you receive your cup, share what you've learned and what you'll take with you."

Before passing the first cup, Elena invited everyone to open their hearts and give gratitude to the spirit of the cacao. "We will practice three mantras here today. The first is: "I wish to open my heart." They all repeated the mantra after her.

Elena then poured the first cup of the rich, dark liquid and passed it to Samantha. As Samantha took the warm cup in her hands, her eyes glistened with unshed tears.

"I came here feeling lost and disconnected from my creativity," Samantha said, her voice thick with emotion. "But through this retreat, I've rediscovered my passion for art. I'm leaving with a renewed sense of purpose and a commitment to prioritize my creative pursuits."

Elena nodded, a pleased smile on her face as she poured the next cup and passed it to Marcus. The usually grumpy executive seemed softer somehow, more open.

"I never thought I'd say this," Marcus began, a hint of wonder in his voice, "but I've learned the value of slowing down. I realize now that my relentless drive was actually holding me back. I'm going to implement mindfulness practices in my daily routine and encourage my team to do the same."

Elena acknowledged Marcus with beaming pride, then led the group into the second mantra: "My heart is opening," which they all repeated.

As Elena handed the third cup to Raj, his eyes sparkled with excitement. "This retreat has reinforced my belief in the power of mindfulness in business," he shared. "I'm going to go even further with what I've already established at my company."

Taylor, usually skeptical and reserved, accepted the fourth cup with a genuine smile. "I came here thinking this was all nonsense," she admitted. "But I'm leaving with a newfound appreciation for vulnerability in leadership. I've realized that showing my human side doesn't make me weak – it makes me a better leader."

"Thank you, Taylor." Let us all repeat now: "My heart is open."

"My heart is open," they said in unison.

Elena poured the last cup of chocolate and handed it to Alex. As he cradled the warm mug, he took a deep breath, feeling the weight of his transformation.

"When I arrived, I was burnt out and like Samantha, disconnected," Alex began, his voice steady but filled with emotion. "But now, I'm leaving with a renewed sense of purpose and a new framework for decision-making. I've learned the importance of creating boundaries, both personal and professional, and I'm committed to leading with more balance and mindfulness."

As Alex finished speaking, Elena looked around the circle, her eyes shining. "I am so proud of each of you," Elena said, her voice filled with warmth. "You've embraced this journey with open hearts and minds, and the growth I've witnessed is truly inspiring. As you return to your lives, remember this moment, this feeling. The lessons you've learned here are not just for this retreat – they're tools for a more balanced, mindful, and fulfilling life."

As they sipped their cacao, which was infused with honey, turmeric, cinnamon, cardamom, and a hint of spearmint, a comfortable silence fell over the group. Each person was lost in reflection, savoring not just the rich flavor of the chocolate, but the profound experiences and insights they had gained. The air was thick with a sense of accomplishment, gratitude, and anticipation for the journey ahead.

Elena reminded them of the additional benefits of cacao, such as its ability to promote neurotransmitters and support emotional well-being. She explained that cacao is often used to move through times of transition and can be a powerful tool for inviting transformation. "But mostly," she added, "I just want to say, welcome home, the home inside yourself."

After the ceremony, the group made their way to the hot tub for a final, celebratory soak. As they relaxed in the warm water, overlooking the stunning lake and volcanoes, there was a bittersweet feeling in the air. They would miss this place, but they were also eager to apply their learnings in the real world.

The final dinner was a joyous affair, filled with laughter, heartfelt toasts, and promises to stay in touch. As Alex looked around the table at his fellow retreat attendees, he marveled at how much they had all changed in just a short time, and even more at how much he had changed himself.

Back in his room, Alex pulled out his journal one last time.

Journal Entry: Day 7 at Oasis del Sol

As I prepare to leave this magical place, I'm filled with gratitude and excitement. Having this time away from work has helped me really clear my head, reassess my approach to life, and filled my heart. To ensure I don't go back to my old ways, I need to make a plan for how to integrate these learnings into my day-to-day approach. Here's what I'm thinking:

1. *Start each day with a short meditation or yoga practice to center myself.*

2. *Implement regular "unplugged" times to disconnect from technology and reconnect with myself and loved ones.*

3. *Practice active listening in meetings, giving my full attention to others.*

4. *Incorporate mindfulness breaks throughout the workday to reset and refocus.*

5. *Prioritize tasks based on importance and impact, not just urgency.*

6. *Set clear boundaries between work and personal time.*

7. *Foster a culture of open communication and vulnerability within my team.*

8. *Regularly reassess and adjust my work-life balance.*

9. *Seek opportunities for continued personal and professional growth.*

10. *Remember to "love the tension" and view challenges as opportunities for growth.*

I know the real test will come when I'm back in the thick of things, but I feel equipped with tools to handle whatever comes my way. This retreat has been transformative, and I'm committed to keeping this energy alive in my daily life.

As Alex closed his journal and began packing his bags, he felt a mix of emotions. There was a tinge of sadness at leaving this peaceful oasis, but it was overshadowed by a sense of excitement and readiness for what lay ahead. He carefully tucked his journal into his carry-on, knowing it would serve as a touchstone in the days and weeks to come.

Setting his alarm for the early morning departure, Alex took one last look out the window at the moonlit lake. He took a deep breath, feeling grounded and centered. Whatever challenges awaited him back home, he knew he was returning as a changed man, ready to lead with newfound wisdom, balance, and purpose.

CHAPTER 11

Homeward Bound

The first light of dawn crept into the rooms at Oasis del Sol, casting a soft glow over the serene landscape. Alex stirred awake, the memories of the previous day's chocolate ceremony still fresh in his mind. He felt a mix of excitement and apprehension as he prepared to leave this transformative place behind.

After a quick breakfast, the group gathered at the dock, where a small boat awaited them. The air was filled with a bittersweet energy as they boarded, each person reflecting on their journey. As the boat glided across the calm waters, Alex took a moment to soak in the beauty of the lake and the majestic volcanoes in the distance, knowing this was a moment he wanted to remember.

Once they reached the shuttle, the atmosphere shifted to one of camaraderie. They shared laughter and stories, each person eager to express gratitude for the connections they had formed. By the time they arrived at the airport, the reality of their departure had sunk in.

"Let's promise to stay in touch," Samantha said, her eyes sparkling with emotion.

"Absolutely," Raj chimed in. "And who knows, maybe we'll be back in a year or two…"

One by one, they exchanged hugs and heartfelt goodbyes, each promising to keep the spirit of the retreat alive in their daily lives. As Alex boarded his flight and settled into his seat, he pulled out his notebook.

With a pen in hand, Alex began to outline his plans for restructuring business operations back at work. He jotted down ideas for implementing mindfulness practices, creating clearer boundaries, and fostering a culture of open communication.

When the plane landed and he stepped into the bustling airport, the familiar sights and sounds felt both comforting and chaotic. As he navigated through the crowd, his heart raced with anticipation. He spotted Olivia near the baggage claim, her eyes scanning the crowd.

The moment their gazes met, something shifted. Without saying a word, she rushed toward him, wrapping her arms around him tightly. Alex felt the warmth of her embrace, grounding him amidst the whirlwind of emotions.

"I missed you," she whispered, pulling back to look into his eyes. In that moment, he could see the relief and joy reflected in her expression. It was as if she could sense the changes within him, the rekindled spark that had dimmed under the weight of work.

"I missed you too," Alex replied, his voice thick with emotion. He realized that he had been holding onto so much during his time away, and now, standing in front of his wife, he felt lighter.

As they walked toward the exit, hand in hand, Alex felt a renewed sense of purpose. He was ready to embrace the challenges ahead, not just as a leader in his company but as a husband and partner. The lessons from Oasis del Sol would guide him, reminding him to find balance, to embrace tension, and to prioritize what truly mattered.

As they stepped out into the cool evening air, Alex felt a deep sense of gratitude for the journey he had undertaken. He was home, and for the first time in a long while, he felt like he had truly returned to himself.

CHAPTER 12

A New Way of Leading

Two months had passed since Alex's return from Oasis del Sol, and the changes were tangible. The office buzzed with a new energy, and Alex found himself at the center of it all.

On this particular morning, Alex arrived at the office early, taking a moment to center himself before the day began. He closed his eyes, took a deep breath, and recalled Elena's words: "Love the tension. It serves a purpose."

As his team filtered in, Alex greeted each person warmly, making eye contact and asking genuine questions about their well-being. Jake, his once-struggling direct report, approached with a confident smile.

"Alex, I've finished the project proposal," Jake said, handing over a folder. "I incorporated some of those mindfulness techniques you suggested. It really helped me focus and think more creatively."

Alex nodded approvingly. "That's great, Jake. I'm looking forward to reviewing it. Let's discuss it over lunch – I'd love to hear more about your process."

Throughout the day, Alex noticed the subtle but significant changes in his team's dynamics. The atmosphere was more relaxed, yet paradoxically, more productive. People seemed more engaged, more willing to share ideas and take calculated risks.

In the afternoon, Alex had a video call with a major client. As he settled into the conference room, he took a moment to ground himself, remembering the importance of being fully present.

"Alex, I have to say, your team's work has been exceptional lately," the client remarked during the call. "There's a noticeable improvement in both the quality and the timeliness of deliverables. What's changed?"

Alex smiled, feeling a surge of pride. "We've implemented some new practices focused on balance and mindfulness," he explained. "It's helping us work smarter, not just harder."

After the call, Alex reviewed the latest performance metrics. The numbers confirmed what he was seeing and feeling:

- Team productivity had increased by 15% over the past two months.

- Client satisfaction scores were up by 20%.

- Employee satisfaction surveys showed a 25% improvement in overall job satisfaction.

- Sick days and stress-related absences had decreased by 30%.

As he looked at these figures, Alex felt a deep sense of satisfaction. The lessons from the retreat weren't just feel-good platitudes – they were translating into real, measurable results.

Later that evening, as Alex prepared to leave the office at a reasonable hour – a new habit he was cultivating – Stephanie from HR stopped by his office.

"Alex, I just wanted to say that the changes you've implemented are really making a difference," she said. "People are happier, more productive, and there's a real sense of purpose in the air. The higher-ups have noticed too."

Alex thanked her, feeling a warmth spread through his chest. As he packed up his things, he glanced at the small potted plant on his desk – a reminder of the serenity he'd found at Oasis del Sol. He smiled, knowing that he had managed to bring a piece of that tranquility into his everyday life.

On his way out, he passed Jake, who was also heading home. "Great job today, Jake," Alex said. "Remember, it's important to disconnect and recharge. The work will be here tomorrow."

Jake nodded appreciatively. "Thanks, Alex. You know, I used to think I needed to work around the clock to impress you. But now I see that balance is what really drives success."

As Alex drove home, he reflected on the journey of the past few months. The transformation hadn't been easy – there had been challenges and moments of doubt. But as he pulled into his driveway, seeing Olivia waiting for him on the porch with a warm smile, he knew that he had found the right path.

He was leading not just with his mind, but with his heart. And in doing so, he had not only improved his team's performance but had also rediscovered the joy in his work and his life. The lessons of Oasis del Sol were not just memories now – they were a living, breathing part of his new approach to leadership and life.

CHAPTER 13

Paying It Forward

Twelve months after his transformative retreat at Oasis del Sol, Alex found himself standing before a room full of eager entrepreneurs at a local business incubator. The nervous energy in the room reminded him of his own struggles not so long ago.

"A year ago," Alex began, "I was where many of you are now. Overwhelmed, stressed, and on the brink of burnout." He paused, letting his words sink in. "But today, I'm here to share how mindfulness changed not just my leadership style, but my entire approach to work and life."

As Alex shared his journey, he could see recognition dawning in the eyes of his audience. He talked about the toll of chronic stress, citing recent research from the American Psychological Association that showed

79% of employees had experienced work-related stress in the month before the survey.

"But here's the good news," Alex continued, his voice filled with hope. "Mindfulness isn't just a buzzword. It's a powerful tool that can significantly reduce burnout and increase productivity."

He went on to explain how implementing mindfulness practices had contributed to a 20% increase in productivity in his own company, surpassing the link between mindfulness training and a 6% increase in task performance shown by researchers.

Inspired by the positive changes in his own life and company, Alex had developed a "Mindful Leadership" program. The program combined the lessons he'd learned at Oasis del Sol with current research on leadership effectiveness and employee well-being.

"This program isn't about becoming a meditation guru," Alex explained. "It's about developing practical skills to manage stress, improve focus, and foster a more positive work environment."

The program included modules on:

1. Mindful Communication: Techniques for active listening and empathetic response

2. Stress Management: Practical mindfulness exercises for the workplace

3. Emotional Intelligence: Developing self-awareness and empathy

4. Mindful Decision Making: Using mindfulness to improve problem-solving skills

As Alex wrapped up his presentation, a young entrepreneur raised her hand. "This all sounds great," she said, "but how do you maintain these practices long-term?"

Alex smiled, appreciating the insightful question. "It's a journey," he replied. "Like any skill, it takes practice. But the benefits – reduced stress, improved relationships, better decision-making – make it worth the effort."

Epilogue

A year after his retreat at Oasis del Sol, Alex stood in his office, looking out over the city skyline. The changes in his life and work were profound and lasting.

His company had seen a 30% reduction in employee turnover, and client satisfaction scores were at an all-time high. Through his leadership at the incubator, The Mindful Leadership program had been implemented in several local businesses, with promising results.

But perhaps the most significant change was in Alex himself. He was calmer, more focused, and more present – both at work and at home. His relationship with Olivia had deepened, and he found joy in the small moments of everyday life.

As he reflected on his journey, Alex remembered a quote from Jon Kabat-Zinn that had become his mantra: "You can't stop the waves, but you can learn to surf."

He smiled, realizing that's exactly what he had learned to do – surf the waves of life and business with grace, resilience, and mindfulness.

Are You Ready to Transform Your Company Culture?

If you're inspired to bring more mindfulness into your organization, I'd love to connect. Let's discuss how we can work together to create a more peaceful, productive, and fulfilling workplace for everyone.

Contact Dr. Sharon Grossman at

www.drsharongrossman.com

Also by Sharon Grossman

About the Author

Dr. Sharon Grossman works with organizations that want to create a thriving corporate culture so their employees feel valued, engaged, and motivated to stay. With over 20 years of experience as a therapist and executive coach, she leverages her psychology background to empower individuals and teams. Dr. Grossman is not only the author of several books including the *Business On the Move* series, but also a sought-after business consultant and keynote speaker.

Through her company, The Productivity Trainers, Dr. Grossman's mission is clear: to guide teams from overwhelmed to optimal performance, all without burning out.

When she's not helping teams reach their full potential, Sharon enjoys life in Miami Beach, Florida with her husband and two children.

Connect with Dr. Sharon:

- Website: www.DrSharonGrossman.com
- LinkedIn: @sharongrossman